Silkk The Shocker's

Written by Silkk The Shocker

Illustrated by Josh Austin

Hey everyone, I'm Coach Shonn and I want to tell you a few things. Firstly and most importantly, YOU ARE SPECIAL! There is only one of you in the entire world. That means that you are unique and no one can replace you. Secondly, your family and friends love you very much! Their world would not be the same without you. Lastly, never let anyone steal your joy! You are smart, strong, and brave! Now that I have reminded you about how awesome you are, I'm going to tell you the story of how my friend Andy found his awesomeness.

Andy was much bigger than most of the kids at his school. He had red hair and pale skin. Because of this his schoolmates gave him the nickname Big Red. He wasn't proud of what made him different and special. Instead he chose to pick on kids that were smaller than him. He used what made him different to bully kids that were too scared to fight back.

Big Red's favorite person to pick on was a kid he called "Little Johnny." Little Johnny was a short, frail, and smart boy with glasses. Big Red would take his lunch money every day. The days that Little Johnny didn't have money to take were the worst. On those days, Big Red would take someone's drink and pour it on Little Johnny.

Big Red had gotten into so much trouble for bullying other kids, that the principal had no choice but to expel him from school.

Big Red had to be enrolled into a new school. On the first day at his new school he realized that the kids were much different from the kids he was used to. Here, Big Red was no longer Big Red. He was actually one of the smallest kids at his new school. Here, he was just the new kid, Andy.

At lunchtime, Andy accidentally bumped into a big kid named Brandon, but everyone in school called him "The Beast." The Beast was much bigger than him. Andy was very scared of him because he was the biggest bully at the school. The Beast demanded Andy give him fifty cents everyday.

For the next couple of weeks, Andy was very lonely. He had a hard time making friends. This made Andy realize how awful he made Johnny feel. Andy began to feel sorry for bullying other kids.

Meanwhile, a girl in Andy's class named Taylor was having problems of her own. She was different, just like Andy. She was short, quirky, and did not wear expensive clothing like her other classmates. Instead of gossiping, she liked to spend her time reading and painting. The two most popular girls in her class, Sierra and Janice, came up to her and began making fun of her. When they became bored of laughing at her they walked away. Taylor was left alone and feeling crushed.

During lunch, Andy came and sat next to Taylor to try and cheer her up. He told her that the girls were probably jealous and intimidated by her because of how special she is. He then confessed to her that he was once a bully. He told her how he would bully kids, not because he did not like them, but because he was jealous of them. He told her about how he bullied Little Johnny because he was one of the teacher's favorite students and how he wanted to be smart like him. Taylor liked his honesty and they became best friends. They then began to hatch a very brave plan.

The next day, The Beast approached Andy for his usual fifty cents at lunch. This time, Andy decided that he had enough of his bully! Andy stood tall and boldly yelled "NO!" to The Beast. The other kids went silent. Andy and The Beast argued back and forth several times. The Beast tried to scare Andy but Andy stayed strong.

When The Beast realized that Andy was no longer going to take his bullying, he walked away in shame and never bothered Andy again.

Taylor was so proud and amazed at Andy's action toward Brandon, that it inspired her to stand up to her bullies!

When the school basketball coach, Coach Shonn, found out what was going on he decided to help take action by organizing an anti-bullying movement. He brought all the kids, parents, teachers, and other members of the community together to do their part to keep the school safe, positive, and bully-free.

In the spirit of forgiveness, Andy told The Beast, who would once again become known only as Brandon, that he wanted to them to be friends. He said that they should put the past behind them because everyone deserves a second chance.
Brandon happily agreed.

One by one, the bullies backed down and the message spread from school to school. The kids made it clear that there were "NO BULLIES ALLOWED"!

Our friend Andy learned to treat others the way you want to be treated. He learned to respect others and in return, he earned the respect of others. It does not matter what other's think about you. You can't truly like someone until you like yourself first. Instead of comparing ourselves to one another we should learn to love what makes us different and celebrate what we have in common. Love yourself because YOU are awesome! Remember that you have friends and family that love and appreciate you, If you need help or someone to talk to, you can reach out to your teacher, coach, parents, siblings, aunts, uncles, grandparents, and friends. There are tons of people around you that care about you because you are AMAZING and UNIQUE, and no one can change that!

About The Author

Vyshonn "Silkk The Shocker" Miller

Multi-platinum recording artist, actor, entertainer, producer and entrepreneur Vyshonn "Silkk" Miller (a.k.a. Silkk The Shocker) knows the importance of a positive influence on our youth. He decided to publish a book series called *Be Better Do Better*. He feels that, since kids are the future, it's necessary to instill and give direction on being the best you can be. With plans to release more books in this series shortly, Silkk's motivation for creating "No Bullies Allowed" was to give a fun, positive voice to the younger generation.

As stated by the author himself, "I see many problems in today's society and I feel it is necessary to express my point of view. One issue I feel very strongly about is bullying. Bullying is a form of abuse that affects everyone involved. By bullying you can damage somebody not only physically, but mentally and emotionally too. It's time we take a stand!"

www.ingramcontent.com/pod-product-compliance
Lightning Source LLC
Chambersburg PA
CBHW040729150426
42811CB00063B/1545